The heart of CHICAGO

MALLARD PRESS
An imprint of BDD Promotional Book Company, Inc.
666 Fifth Avenue,
New York, N.Y. 10103

Mallard Press and its accompanying duck logo are
registered trademarks of
BDD Promotional Book Company, Inc.
Registered in the U.S. Patent and Trademark Office.
CLB 3162
© 1993 Colour Library Books Ltd.,
Godalming, Surrey, England
First published in the United States of America 1993
by The Mallard Press
Printed and bound in Singapore
All rights reserved
ISBN 0 7924 5828 1

The heart of
CHICAGO

Text by
PAM ADKINS

MALLARD
PRESS

In September 1871, Chicagoans had something new to talk about besides the weather, which had been hot and dry since June. Their brand-new baseball team, the White Stockings, had just knocked the socks off the Cincinnati Red Stockings, and nearly half the town turned out to give them a hearty welcome home. It didn't seem likely that anything more important could possibly happen to make 1871 a historic year for Chicago, but there were some, or so they claimed years later, who knew better.

The ones who said that they had seen it coming were mostly preachers, and their followers were given to handwringing over what was becoming of the lusty former trading post between Lake Michigan and the prairie. It had attracted so many gamblers, confidence men, prostitutes, pickpockets and thieves that they had had to create suburbs to contain them. And upstanding citizens who were forced to step over drunks on their way to church nodded their heads in agreement when the man in the pulpit thundered that God would eventually have to take matters into His own hands.

The Lord works in mysterious ways, and the mystery of how He dealt with Chicago has never really been solved. Most people blamed a cow, but the animal's owner, Mrs. Catherine O'Leary, denied it to her dying day. And whether a cow kicked over a lantern or the Almighty hurled a thunderbolt into the O'Leary hayloft was the least of anybody's problems on the night of October 8, 1871. Within a few hours, all of Chicago's West Side was in flames, and by morning the fire had spread to the entire city. Before it was over, thirty-one hours after it began, 17,450 buildings that had filled three-and-a-half square miles were gone. One hundred thousand people were homeless and, though officials estimated that two hundred and fifty were dead, it was probably at least twice that number. Put together, the Great Fire of London in 1666 and the 1835 fire that destroyed downtown New York did less damage.

Among the losses that included cash in bank vaults and a million-and-a-half dollars in the Customs House, for which the collector in charge was held personally responsible, were all the records of who owned what parcels of land. When the Court House collapsed, every document inside was reduced to fine ash. Fortunately, abstracts of deeds and land titles were saved by John Shortall, a partner in a firm that kept such records, who also helped one of his competitors move his files from the path of the fire. Just as fortuitously, one of the city's leading architects, John Van Osdel, managed to save his drawings by burying them under wet clay in the basement of the new Palmer House Hotel. It gave him a decided edge in rebuilding the city when he claimed to be able to duplicate any lost building in just a few months.

With banks able to lend money without fear of lawsuits over land claims, and architects set to move quickly, the rebuilding of Chicago began before the ruins had cooled. The business district was back in business within a year, and in three years there were almost no signs that there had ever been a fire. Van Osdel's discovery that baked clay – terra cotta – was a good fireproofing material, and the fact that Otto Matz's Nixon Building survived the fire because he had coated its wrought iron beams with concrete and plaster of Paris, gave a fireproof feeling to the new city, but by and large it was a hodge-podge of architectural styles. And not only was there no attempt to take advantage of an opportunity to create a harmonious cityscape, but architects were so eager to get on to the next project and another fee of one-and-a-half percent of a building's cost, they cut corners in safety, too. Another disaster seemed to be waiting to happen, but when it came it was in the form of a national depression.

But, like the fire, the downturn turned out to be good, not only for Chicago but for most of the cities of the world. It was the incubation period of the Chicago School of architecture. During the six-year depression beginning in 1873, young architects like Louis Sullivan and Dankmar Adler, Daniel Burnham and John Root, who had no memories of the pre-fire city and little use for the forms their competitors were using to replace it, began thinking about what form cities of the future should take. They had a few role models, the most notable of which was William L. Jenney's 1872 Portland Block, a solid brick structure without the clutter of borrowed style, which, like Matz's Nixon Building, depended on its own mass to make a statement. Such ideas made good sense, and when the depression ended Adler and Sullivan built the Borden Block, and Burnham and Root followed it with their Grannis and Montauk Blocks, and the message was sent all over the world that ornamentation was passé, and that light and

First page: the Chicago skyline. Previous page: the Sears Tower, rising high above Chicago's other skyscrapers. Left: the Standard Oil Building, known affectionately as "Old Stan."

space and a building's own structure were all that were important. As Louis Sullivan explained it, "form follows function."

Their clients also had a hand in the new architects' vision. In the past they had demanded that office and retail buildings should reflect their own stability, and the answer, ironically, had been to create monuments to the lost civilizations of Greece and Rome. But by the 1880s, with the development of safe elevators, it was clear that the best way to make a building profitable on expensive land was to make it taller. However, there was little precedent either in the ancient world or in the recent past to stretch architectural elements over more than three or four stories in height, and the demand brought engineering headaches, too. When Burnham and Root were commissioned to build the Montauk, their clients, Boston businessmen Peter and Shepard Brooks, demanded a ten-story building. The architects accepted the challenge, but they knew they had a problem. The combined weight of brick and stone piled that high could make a building sink into the ground almost in direct proportion to its reach for the sky, especially in a place like Chicago, which less than fifty years earlier was a marsh, hard-pressed to support anything heavier than acres of wild onions.

John Root solved the problem by resting the base of the building on a thick concrete slab reinforced with iron rails, which he characterized as a "floating raft." With its weight distributed evenly, the architects produced the requested ten-story building, often called the first of the world's skyscrapers, and the Brookses were so pleased that they ordered another, the 16-story Monadnock, built in 1891.

In the meantime, another Bostonian, Henry Hobson Richardson, had built a Romanesque warehouse for Marshall Field that impressed Louis Sullivan enough for him to comment that it caused "stone and mortar to spring to life." Following Richardson's example, he created the Auditorium Building, and from then on Sullivan was the man to follow among architects and others who believed that big buildings should enrich a city. Also impressed by Richardson's mastery, Burnham and Root took his ideas another step forward when they built the massive but graceful Rookery, and by 1890 it was clear that America finally had its own architectural signature and that its flourish was

in Chicago. It was an accomplishment as unprecedented as the buildings themselves. The creators were all in their early thirties and, except for Sullivan, none had studied in Europe, which was up to that time considered the most important credential an architect could have. Richardson's presence among them gave them a benchmark, but their approach to building Chicago was a complete break with the past, and the clean slate they started with helped them refine what is still one of the world's most orderly cities.

New generations of architects would eventually be inspired by what the Chicagoans accomplished in the 1880s, but their well-established contemporaries weren't quite so sure that these upstarts had discovered the key to the future. They were given their chance to make their own statements in 1893, and when they had finished, Louis Sullivan said that "The damage wrought … will last for half a century."

The perpetrators were some of the giants of American Architecture: Richard Morris Hunt, Charles Follen McKim, Stanford White, George B. Post and a half dozen others working with such artists as sculptors Daniel Chester French and Frederick MacMonnies. It all prompted Augustus St. Gaudens, himself one of the great sculptors of modern times, to say that "This is the greatest gathering of artists since the fifteenth century." In Chicago, no less! He was right, of course, but the problem was that Chicago's own creative genius was all but ignored.

It didn't start out that way. When a movement began to mark the four-hundredth anniversary of the discovery of America, Chicago fought for and won the right to be the host city of the World's Columbian Exposition. There was no denying it would be good for business, but it would also be a perfect showcase for the city's architects. With that in mind, John Root and Daniel Burnham were named its architectural directors. The only Easterner involved at the beginning was Frederick Law Olmstead, the landscape designer who had created New York's Central Park. But he had also made his mark in Chicago by planning its ring of municipal parks and its tree-lined boulevards. Once they agreed on Jackson Park, overlooking Lake Michigan, as the site, Root and Olmstead designed an assemblage of lagoons, reflecting pools and canals surrounded by a circle of formal buildings.

Right: a variety of pleasure boats moored at Burnham Park Yacht Harbor, situated close to Merrill C. Meigs Airport.

What they called the Court of Honor turned out to be the Trojan Horse of the Fair.

Root invited the Eastern architects to contribute the ring of structures that would recall the past, and decided to commission the rest among the creators of the Chicago School as a showcase for the future. But when the Chicagoans got together to discuss their participation, John Wellborn Root was not at the meeting. He was ill with pneumonia, and four days later he was dead. The mantle passed to Daniel Burnham, who was more of a realist than an idealist and, responding to pressure from the business community, he replaced his former partner with a representative of the Eastern establishment, Charles B. Attwood. With a member of the Old School rather than one of the Chicago School setting the standard, the Exposition became a Beaux Arts fantasy of classical columns, garlands and statues. Columbus himself would have been pleased, and so were most Americans. It started the so-called City Beautiful Movement that put classical columns and domes on public buildings, banks, museums and libraries all over the country, from Washington, DC to Chicago itself. But it wasn't the contribution Chicago architects had hoped to make. The most notable local statements made at the 1893 Columbian Exposition were Adler and Sullivan's Transportation Building and Henry Ives Cobb's Fisheries Building. Even William Jenney, whose personal interest was in solving engineering problems rather than aesthetics, bowed to the Beaux Arts style with the great glass dome of his Horticultural Hall.

But the Chicago School had enough functioning examples of its own style in the city proper, and the message wasn't completely lost. The Fair, after all, was just a stage set and everyone knew it. The theater itself was the important thing and fairgoers were quite impressed by what Chicago had accomplished, and they didn't detect a trace of boosterism when the mayor predicted that one day soon "New York shall say: 'Let us go to the metropolis of America!'."

A century later, New Yorkers still look nervously over their shoulders, not to see if Chicago is getting bigger, but if it is getting better. And there are some among them who privately admit – very quietly – that it has.

The 1893 Fair also confirmed what everyone already knew, and what is still quite true: that Chicagoans know how to have a good time. One of the reasons why it was chosen was that its population was such a representative cross-section of America, which prompted a class-conscious critic to make what could be an appropriate remark for the politically-correct 1990s. "An exposition to honor who?," he sniffed. "Christopher Columbus? In a social way, Columbus was an ordinary man." If he was, he'd have loved the show Chicago put on in his memory.

For openers, it had a crowd-pleaser in the person of a belly dancer known as Little Egypt. In a society that found an occasional flash of a feminine ankle a moving experience, a navel in motion was probably more memorable than the greatest number of electric lights ever seen in one place up until that time. The lights outlined all the buildings and made the fountains a riot of changing colors in what many said was more spectacular than the Chicago fire itself. Mrs. Potter Palmer, who served as the Fair's social director and used it as a platform to champion her crusade for women's rights, allowed the belly dancer's show to go on when it was pointed out that Little Egypt was demonstrating a religious ritual thousands of years old.

Cultural uplift was also a possible explanation for the thrill of sitting in a gondola suspended between a pair of giant wheels created by George Washington Gale Ferris especially for the Fair. When they reached the top, two-hundred-and-fifty feet up, passengers could see all the way to the heart of the city, seven miles to the north. But there were all sorts of cultures to be sampled right there on the ground. The Egyptian exhibit offered camel rides and Vienna contributed an orchestra for outdoor waltzing. Thrillseekers could kiss a Blarney Stone in an Irish castle; a heady experience even if the stone wasn't the real McCoy. There was a full-size representation of the Venus de Milo in solid milk chocolate and another, also life-size, of the governor of Montana in solid silver. One exhibit featured a Bell telephone that could be used to call New York if anyone cared to, and the Liberty Bell had been shipped in from Philadelphia to add a proper patriotic note to the proceedings. John Philip Sousa was there with his band, and the two-year-old Chicago Symphony Orchestra was on hand for a series of outdoor

Left: the Sun-Times Building – housing the offices of one of the city's most popular papers – the Wrigley Tower and the Tribune Tower.

concerts. And, in another corner, Gentleman Jim Corbett was giving demonstrations of the knockout punch that surprised the great John L. Sullivan. Sandow, the world's strongest man, showed what could be accomplished with a little daily exercise, and America's first disciple of physical fitness, Bernard McFadden, was there with the right advice for anyone in search of the body beautiful, the most famous of which belonged to Lillian Russell in those days. She was appearing downtown at the Columbia Theater that summer and was frequently seen at the Fair on the arm of Diamond Jim Brady, and the women's rights crusader, Susan B. Anthony, provided a perfect counterpoint to the message Lil and Jim were flaunting. But even the Archbishop of Ireland, one of a long list of the Fair's distinguished guests, couldn't help smiling when Ms. Anthony told her audience that she was going to start a prayer vigil to drive demon rum from the land Columbus had discovered.

Of course, her prayers were answered nearly thirty years later, and Prohibition put Chicago on the map again thanks to a struggle among local gangsters for control of the beer and booze market in a thirsty city. But that, like the fire and the Fair, is all in the past. More important as a legacy of Chicago's past is the work of its architects. If Louis Sullivan's influence was slow to take root in his own country, his ideas quickly spread to Europe, and the work of his student, Frank Lloyd Wright, and his Prairie School of architecture revolutionized residential housing, not only in Chicago's suburbs but all over the United States. And during the period gangsters were shooting each other on Chicago's streets, Daniel Burnham's plan for redesigning the city was beginning to bear fruit with the widening of Michigan

Avenue and the addition of dozens of limestone skyscrapers that were the envy of the world, among them Graham, Anderson, Probst and White's Wrigley Building. From the day it was finished in 1921, the tower on the river has been every Chicagoan's favorite, and nothing built before or since has quite reflected the spirit of the city in the same way.

The Chicago School influenced the rest of the world, and in the 1930s European architects escaping the Nazis naturally gravitated there. Chief among them was Ludwig Mies van der Rohe, who brought the International Style to America and made glass the material of choice for enclosing elegant skyscrapers. The message was lost on most of Mies's imitators, who put glass boxes everywhere in the 1950s, but among his Chicago buildings, the Lake Shore Drive Apartments, the Federal Center and the IBM Building showed the world how it ought to be done. His successors, Skidmore, Owings and Merrill, took his theories a step further with the Richard Daley Center and Chicago's tallest buildings, the 95-story John Hancock Center and the 110-story Sears Tower, the tallest building in the world.

It's entirely appropriate that the biggest skyscraper is in Chicago, where the idea first started. But Chicago is more than a city of impressive buildings reaching for the sky. Up and down the lake it is more exciting and cosmopolitan than any city in the world, but just a few blocks from the shore it suddenly becomes a small town with a human scale most other cities envy. The late Senator Paul Douglas, who loved the city as much as anyone, summed it up when he said that "Chicago is a town with a Queen Anne front and a Mary Anne back." It may be why other boosters are proud to say that Chicago is a city that works.

The distinctive 1930s skyscrapers (right) are as much a part
of Chicago's skyline as their modern counterparts.

19

Chicago's famed skyline (left) is dominated by the magnificent, 110-story Sears Tower. Reaching a height of 1,454 feet, the distinctive black building soars above the city's other skyscrapers. The views from the Skydeck, which is situated on the 103d floor, are breathtaking. Right: a panoramic view of the city, looking north from the Sears Tower.

333 Wacker Drive (left) is undoubtedly the most unusual of the city's skyscrapers. The building, designed by William Pedersen and completed in the mid-1980s, is simple and understated in its elegance. Above: the Sears Tower, the world's tallest building, dwarfs the skyscrapers surrounding it.

The John Hancock Center (left), known fondly by Chicagoans as "Big John," is one of the city's landmarks. The distinctive tower, with its tapering walls, rises over 1,100 feet above the ground and dominates all other buildings in the immediate vicinity. Right: the magnificent Wrigley Building, the most ornate of the buildings on Michigan Avenue.

Those who make the short journey from the heart of
downtown Chicago to Burnham Park Yacht Harbor (these
pages) are rewarded with fine views of the city skyline.

The contrast between the city's old and new is more apparent at night when the buildings are illuminated (these pages). Right: nighttime traffic at the intersection of West Wacker Drive and Dearborn.

333 Wacker Drive and the Sears Tower (left), two of Chicago's most famous landmarks, represent very different styles of architecture and are a "must see" for any visitor to the city. The Water Tower (right), situated at Michigan and Chicago avenues, is one of the city's most historic buildings. The gothic-style structure was one of the few buildings to survive the fire of 1871.

Marina City (left), a pair of sixty-story circular towers situated on Dearborn, by the banks of the Chicago River, contain apartments, shopping centers and offices. Their unusual design makes the towers among the city's most easily identifiable landmarks. Right: the city skyline seen from the Chicago River. Overleaf: the city's "giants" seen from the south east.

The Buckingham Memorial Fountain (these pages), located
at the center of Grant Park, was built in 1927 in memory of
Clarence Buckingham by his sister Kate.

These pages: the Spanish Renaissance-style Wrigley Building dominates the Michigan Avenue Bridge and the "Magnificent Mile," a sophisticated neighborhood of fine shops and museums.

From 9.30 am when trading begins, activity on the Trading Floor of the Chicago Board of Trade (these pages) is frantic. Established in 1848, it is the largest commodities futures market in the United States, dealing in both agricultural and non-agricultural goods.

In Chicago's Chinatown (left) Oriental architecture dominates. Right: the colorful Mexican Parade, on Dearborn.

The view of Chicago's skyline from Burnham Park Yacht Harbor (these pages) brings the height and variety of the city's skyscrapers into perspective. Right: the magnificent Sears Tower, the undisputed monarch of the city. Overleaf: a golden sunset over Burnham Park Yacht Harbor.

These pages: bright lights illuminate the city center at
night, bringing vibrancy and color to the most ordinary of
streets and lending magic to city landmarks such as the
Wrigley Building (right).

Left: the distinctive Associates Building, on north Michigan Avenue. Right: beautiful Grant Park, famed for its rose gardens, is one of the parks that line the shores of Lake Michigan, offering moments of peace and tranquillity away from the bustling city.

The Loop (these pages), an elevated railroad constructed in the 1890s, encircles Chicago's historic business district. The name has now become synonymous with this part of town.

Right: Marina City, seen from within The Loop, an area of downtown Chicago named for the elevated railroad that has served it since the 1890s. Left: a view down Michigan Avenue.

Expensive boutiques and famous designer shops (left) line Chicago's prestigious Michigan Avenue. Above: the Contemporary American Art Room, at the Art Institute of Chicago, one of the fine museums located on Michigan Avenue.

These pages: nighttime in Chicago, the home of the skyscraper, is spectacular. Lights glitter in the windows of the city's giants, stretching as far as the eye can see.

Right: the ornate floor of the State of Illinois Center, one of the buildings of which the city is justly proud. Above: the United Airlines Terminal at O'Hare Airport, the world's busiest international airport.

The Adler Planetarium (left), located at the southern end of Grant Park, is numbered among Chicago's top ten sightseeing attractions. The planetarium, originally funded by Max Adler, a former vice president of Sears Roebuck & Company, explores the wonders of the universe. Right: "Flamingo," one of Chicago's avant garde pieces of civic architecture. Overleaf: Lake Shore Drive.

Left: colorful paintwork contrasts with the gloom of the
public thoroughfare under the "E" tracks, on Chicago
Avenue north. Above: a peaceful moment by the fountain
outside the Wrigley Building.

The Field Museum of Natural History (these pages), in Grant Park, was built between 1915 and 1920 with funds donated by Marshall Field I, founder of the Marshall Field & Company retail stores. In the museum's imposing entrance hall stand two stuffed elephants and the skeleton of a dinosaur.

The Loop, the elevated railroad that encircles Chicago's
business district, runs high above the city's streets (above).
Like the series of lift bridges that cross the Chicago River
(right), The Loop is one of features of the city.

The State of Illinois Center (right) is just one example of the innovative architecture found in Chicago. Like its buildings, the city's civic sculpture is among the most avant garde in the world. In Daley Plaza stands a massive 50-foot-tall sculpture (left), which was given as a gift to the city by the artist Pablo Picasso.

The Chicago Mercantile Exchange (these pages and overleaf)
is one of three futures exchanges found in the city. It was
established in 1919 and traded primarily in agricultural
commodities until the 1970s. The Exchange moved to its
present address on Wacker Drive in 1983.

The George Washington, Robert Morris, and Haym Salomon Memorial (left) in Heald Square was presented to the City of Chicago in 1941. The monument, designed by American sculptor Lorado Taft, commemorates three of the nation's greatest patriots. Right: the statue of the Swedish botanist Linné.

Even a short journey down Lake Shore Drive (left) brings ample rewards. The drive follows the shores of Lake Michigan for 124 blocks, offering fine views of the city, its parks, and of the lake itself. Right: a view down busy Michigan Avenue, towards Lake Michigan.

When the first skyscrapers started to take shape in the nineteenth century, innovative and experimental architecture was the order of the day. This legacy is still apparent in buildings such as the Sears Tower (left) and 333 Wacker Drive (right). Overleaf: a panorama of the city and its lake shore.

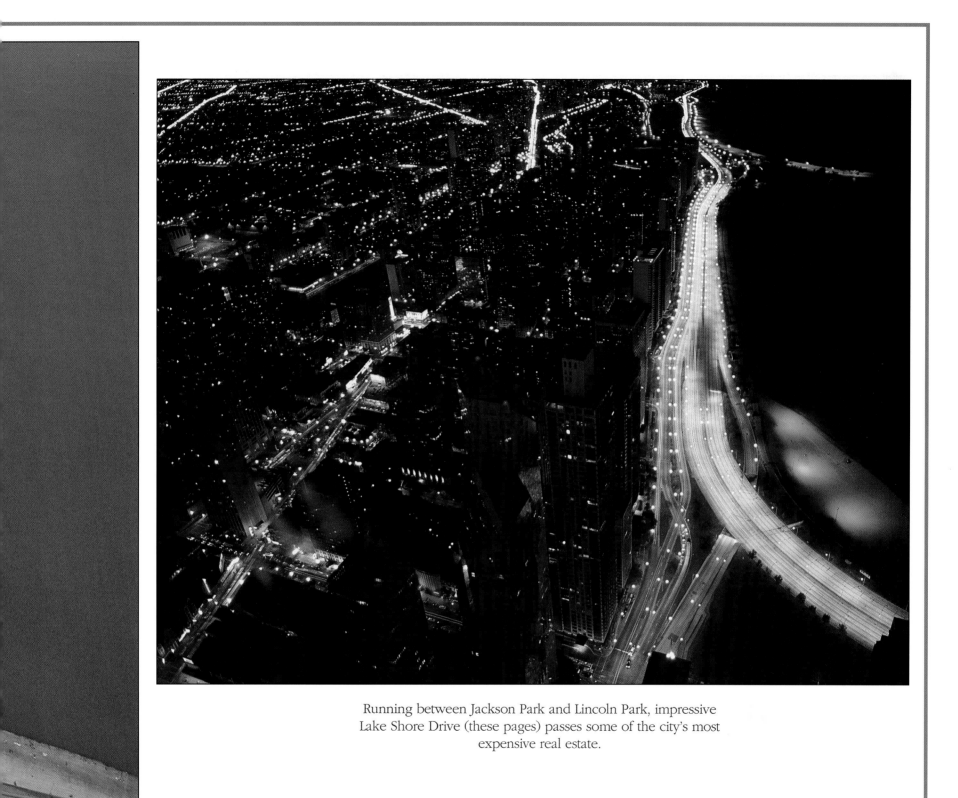

Running between Jackson Park and Lincoln Park, impressive
Lake Shore Drive (these pages) passes some of the city's most
expensive real estate.

Colored lights dazzle the eye in nighttime Chicago, illuminating the store front (left) and adding softness to the rush of water of Buckingham Fountain.

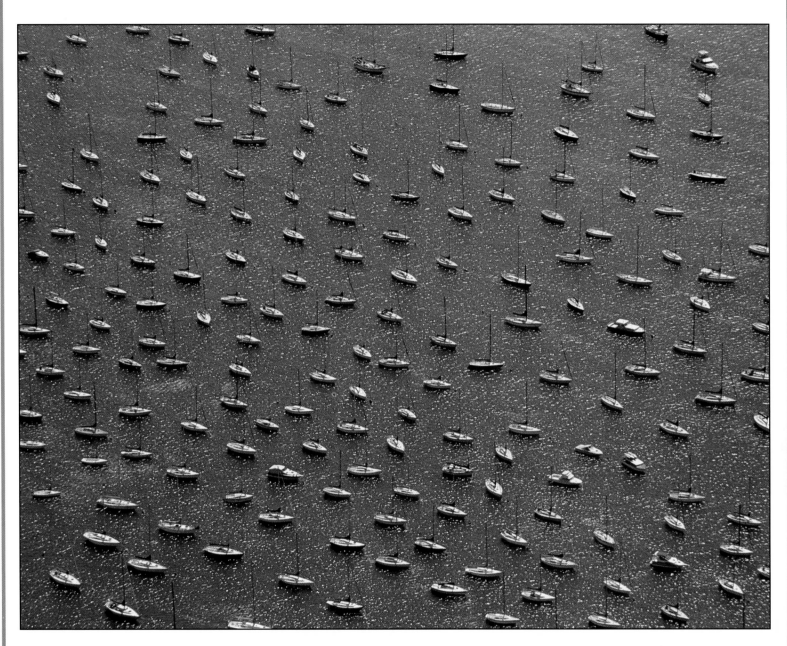

With Lake Michigan right on the doorstep, it is hardly surprising that sailing is a popular recreational activity. Monroe St. Harbor (above) is just one of the moorings available to the yachtsmen. Right: an aerial view of the city, looking across Monroe St. Harbor and Grant Park.

Elaborate patterns of light, like that on the IBM Building (left), are only part of the spectacle of Chicago after dark. Lights glitter from the windows of every skyscraper, and can be seen stretching far into the distance (right).

At night, Chicago becomes a mass of gleaming lights (these pages). Famous city landmarks like the Wrigley Building, Tribune Tower, and the Equitable Life Building (left) are illuminated, providing points of bearing.

The 1869 Gothic-style Water Tower and Pumping Station on Michigan Avenue (right) were among the few survivors of the great fire of 1871. Though the Pumping Station still serves its original function, the Water Tower has been converted into a tourist information center. Left: the sleek, white United Insurance Building.

The George Washington, Robert Morris, and Haym Salomon Memorial (left), a magnificent bronze standing in Heald Square, was designated a Chicago Landmark in 1971. The Hall of Fame at the Merchandise Mart (right), on Lake Shore Drive, is another of the city's monuments to famous men.

The Chicago River (these pages), cuts through the city from east to west. Of the 53 moveable bridges that span the river, Michigan Avenue Bridge (left) is probably the most famous. The double-decked bridge was constructed in 1920, and was an important factor in the subsequent development of Michigan Avenue North as a shopping area. Overleaf: Burnham Park Yacht Harbor.

Above: a train speeds into downtown Chicago from the
East Side. Left: a spectacular aerial view of the city.

"Big John," as the John Hancock Center (left) is known by locals, is the fifth tallest building in the world. The building dwarfs the historic Water Tower, which is located at the intersection of Chicago and Michigan avenues. Right: the distinctive form of the Sears Tower, rising above the city skyline at night.

Above: the Wrigley Building which was designed so that to anyone in Michigan Avenue south of the river it would seem as if the building were standing in the middle of the road. Right and overleaf: Chicago's high-rises silhouetted against the dark sky. Following page: a view of the city from Lake Michigan.